TRADITIONAL SONGS

The Wheels on the Bus

Edited by Ann Owen
Illustrated by Sandra D'Antonio

PICTURE WINDOW BOOKS
MINNEAPOLIS, MINNESOTA

Music Consultant: Peter Mercer-Taylor, Ph.D.
Associate Professor of Musicology
University of Minnesota,
Minneapolis, Minnesota

Reading Consultant: Susan Kesselring, M.A.
Literacy Educator
Rosemount-Apple Valley-Eagan
(Minnesota) School District

Traditional Songs series editor: Peggy Henrikson
Page production: The Design Lab
Musical arrangement: Elizabeth Temple
The illustrations in this book were rendered in pen with digital coloring.

PICTURE WINDOW BOOKS
5115 Excelsior Boulevard
Suite 232
Minneapolis, MN 55416
1-877-845-8392
www.picturewindowbooks.com

Printed in the United States of America.
1 2 3 4 5 6 08 07 06 05 04 03

Library of Congress Cataloging-in-Publication Data
The wheels on the bus / edited by Ann Owen ; illustrated by Sandra D'Antonio.
p. cm. — (Traditional songs)
Summary: Presents an illustrated version of the traditional song along with some
discussion of its folk origins.
Includes bibliographical references (p.   ).
ISBN 1-4048-0154-5 (library binding)
1. Folk songs, English—United States—History and criticism—Juvenile literature.
2. Children's songs, English—United States—History and criticism—Juvenile literature.
3. Children's songs—Texts. [1. Buses—Songs and music. 2. Songs. 3. Finger play.]
I. Owen, Ann, 1953– II. D'Antonio, Sandra, 1956– ill. III. Series.
ML3551 .W475 2003
782.42162'13'00268—dc21
2002155293

What do you see when you sing a song? Does the music come in colors?

What do you do when you sing a song? Does the melody make you dance?

What do you hear when you sing a song? Do the words tell a story?

Let's explore the sights and sounds of one of our favorite songs.

Here comes the bus!

Look for the action cues in the song.

The wheels on the bus go round and round,
round and round, round and round.

The wheels on the bus go round and round,
all around the town.

The wipers on the bus go
swish swish swish,
swish swish swish,
swish swish swish.
The wipers on the bus go
swish swish swish,
all around the town.

The driver on the bus goes "Move on back!
Move on back, move on back!"

The driver on the bus goes
"Move on back!" all around the town.

The people on the bus
go up and down,
up and down, up and down.
The people on the bus
go up and down,
all around the town.

The horn on the bus goes beep beep beep,

beep beep beep, beep beep beep.
The horn on the bus goes beep beep beep,
all around the town.

The kids on the bus go "Yak yak yak,
yak yak yak, yak yak yak."
The kids on the bus go "Yak yak yak,"
all around the town.

15

The baby on the bus goes "Wah wah wah, wah wah wah, wah wah wah." The baby on the bus goes "Wah wah wah," all around the town.

The parents on the bus go "Shh shh shh,
shh shh shh, shh shh shh."
The parents on the bus go "Shh shh shh,"
all around the town.

The wheels on the bus go round and round,
round and round, round and round.
The wheels on the bus go round and round,
all around the town.

The Wheels on the Bus

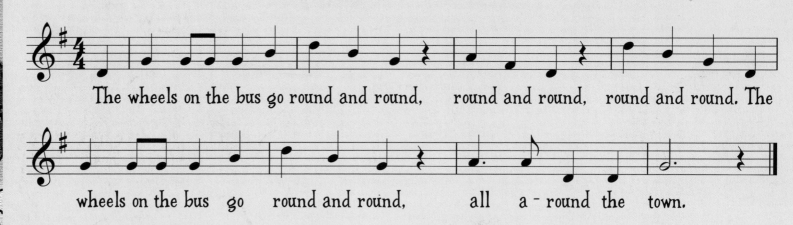

The wheels on the bus go round and round, round and round, round and round. The

wheels on the bus go round and round, all a-round the town.

2. The wipers on the bus go swish swish swish,
Swish swish swish, swish swish swish.
The wipers on the bus go swish swish swish,
All around the town.

3. The driver on the bus goes "Move on back!
Move on back, move on back!"
The driver on the bus goes "Move on back!"
All around the town.

4. The people on the bus go up and down,
Up and down, up and down.
The people on the bus go up and down,
All around the town.

5. The horn on the bus goes beep beep beep,
Beep beep beep, beep beep beep.
The horn on the bus goes beep beep beep,
All around the town.

6. The kids on the bus go "Yak yak yak,
Yak yak yak, yak yak yak."
The kids on the bus go "Yak yak yak,"
All around the town.

7. The baby on the bus goes "Wah wah wah,
Wah wah wah, wah wah wah."
The baby on the bus goes "Wah wah wah,"
All around the town.

8. The parents on the bus go "Shh shh shh,
Shh shh shh, shh shh shh."
The parents on the bus go "Shh shh shh,"
All around the town.

9. The wheels on the bus go round and round,
Round and round, round and round.
The wheels on the bus go round and round,
All around the town.

About the Song

"The Wheels on the Bus" is sometimes called "The Bus Song." This song first came out in songbooks in the early 1960s. Like many folk tunes, no one knows who wrote it. "The Wheels on the Bus" is similar to an older song, "Old MacDonald Had a Farm." Both songs are examples of what is called an imitation song. They are called imitation songs because different sounds are imitated, or copied, in the songs.

DID YOU KNOW?

The first city bus service in the United States began about 1830 in New York City. The buses didn't look like the buses we have today. These buses were made of wood and pulled by horses. They looked more like large stagecoaches. People could ride both inside and on the roof. Motors were put in buses in the early 1900s.

23

Make a Musical Instrument: Rhythm Shaker

WHAT YOU NEED:

- potato chip can (tube style) with lid
- construction paper
- scissors
- crayons or markers
- glue or tape
- aluminum foil: two pieces, each about 6 inches by 15 inches (15 centimeters by 38 centimeters)
- dried beans, unpopped popcorn, or rice (about two spoonfuls)

WHAT TO DO:

1. Take the lid off a clean, empty potato chip can.
2. Trim a sheet of construction paper to fit around the can.
3. Decorate the paper by drawing designs with crayons or markers.
4. Glue or tape the paper around the can.
5. Crunch and roll each piece of aluminum foil into a snake shape, then twist each one into a coil to look like a spring.
6. Put the foil pieces into the tube.
7. Pour the beans, rice, or popcorn into the tube.
8. Put the lid on, and you are ready to shake!

To Learn More

AT THE LIBRARY

Cohn, Amy L. *From Sea to Shining Sea: A Treasury of American Folklore and Folk Songs.* New York: Scholastic, 1993.

Hort, Lenny. *The Seals on the Bus.* New York: Henry Holt, 2000.

Krull, Kathleen. *Gonna Sing My Head Off!: American Folk Songs for Children.* New York: A. A. Knopf, 1992.

Ready, Dee. *School Buses.* Mankato, Minn.: Bridgestone Books, 1998.

Yolen, Jane. *Jane Yolen's Old MacDonald Songbook.* Honesdale, Pa.: Boyds Mills Press, 1994.

Zelinsky, Paul O. *The Wheels on the Bus.* New York: Dutton Children's Books, 1990.

ON THE WEB

CHILDREN'S MUSIC WEB
http://www.childrensmusic.org
For resources and links on children's music for kids, parents, educators, and musicians

NATIONAL INSTITUTE OF ENVIRONMENTAL HEALTH SCIENCES KIDS' PAGES: CHILDREN'S SING-ALONG SONGS
http://www.niehs.nih.gov/kids/musicchild.htm
For music and lyrics to many favorite, traditional children's songs

FACT HOUND
Want more information about traditional songs? FACT HOUND offers a safe, fun way to find Web sites. All of the sites on Fact Hound have been researched by our staff. Simply follow these steps:

1. Visit *http://www.facthound.com.*
2. Enter a search word or 1404801545.
3. Click Fetch It.

Your trusty Fact Hound will fetch the best sites for you!